Copyright © 2024 by Waqas Amin.

All rights reserved. No part of this book may be reproduced, stored, or transmitted in any form or by any means—electronic, mechanical, photocopying, recording, or otherwise—without prior written permission of the publisher.

First Edition, December 2024

ISBN: 979-8-3037-2423-5

Cover Design by Waqas Amin
Printed in the United Kingdom

ZAKARIYYA'S DINO ADVENTURE

Once upon a time, in a quiet little town, lived a curious 5-year-old boy named Zakariyya. He loved exploring, asking questions and learning new things. But most of all, Zakariyya loved dinosaurs!

One sunny morning, Zakariyya's Daddy gave him a special gift—a book about dinosaurs. "JazakAllahu Khair, Daddy!" Zakariyya said with a big smile. He opened the book and saw amazing pictures of giant creatures.

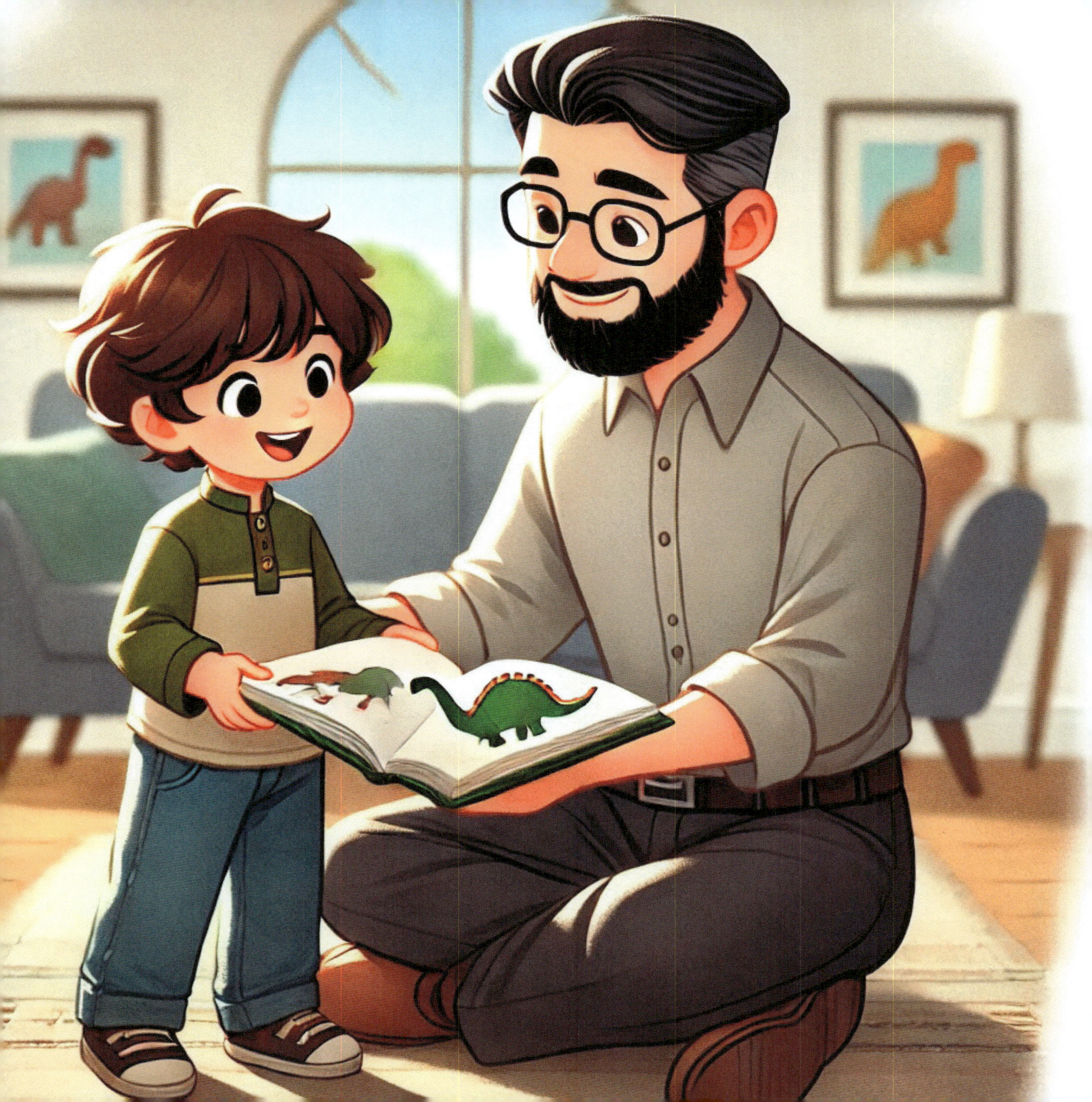

Suddenly, something magical happened! The pages of the book began to glow, shining brighter and brighter. Zakariyya stared in amazement as the words on the page swirled around like tiny dancing stars.

Before he could say a word, he felt a gentle breeze. He blinked, and just like that, he wasn't in his room anymore! Zakariyya looked around and gasped. He was standing in a beautiful jungle full of giant trees, colorful plants, and... dinosaurs!

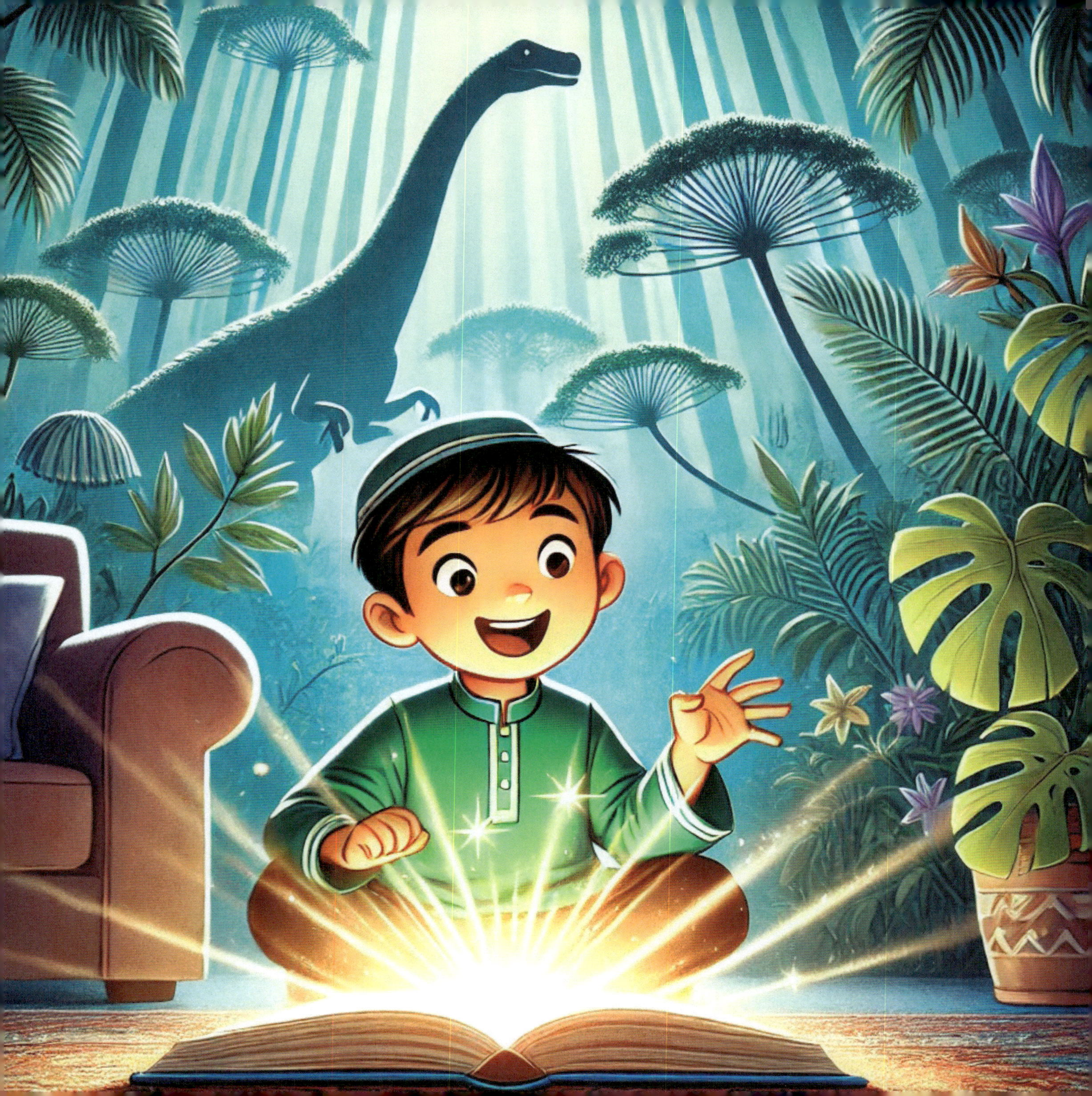

"SubhanAllah! Look at all the dinosaurs!" Zakariyya whispered in awe.

He took a few steps forward, feeling the soft grass under his feet. A group of colorful birds with tiny wings fluttered past him, chirping happily. Zakariyya couldn't believe his eyes. Some dinosaurs were as small as goats, while others were as tall as buildings!

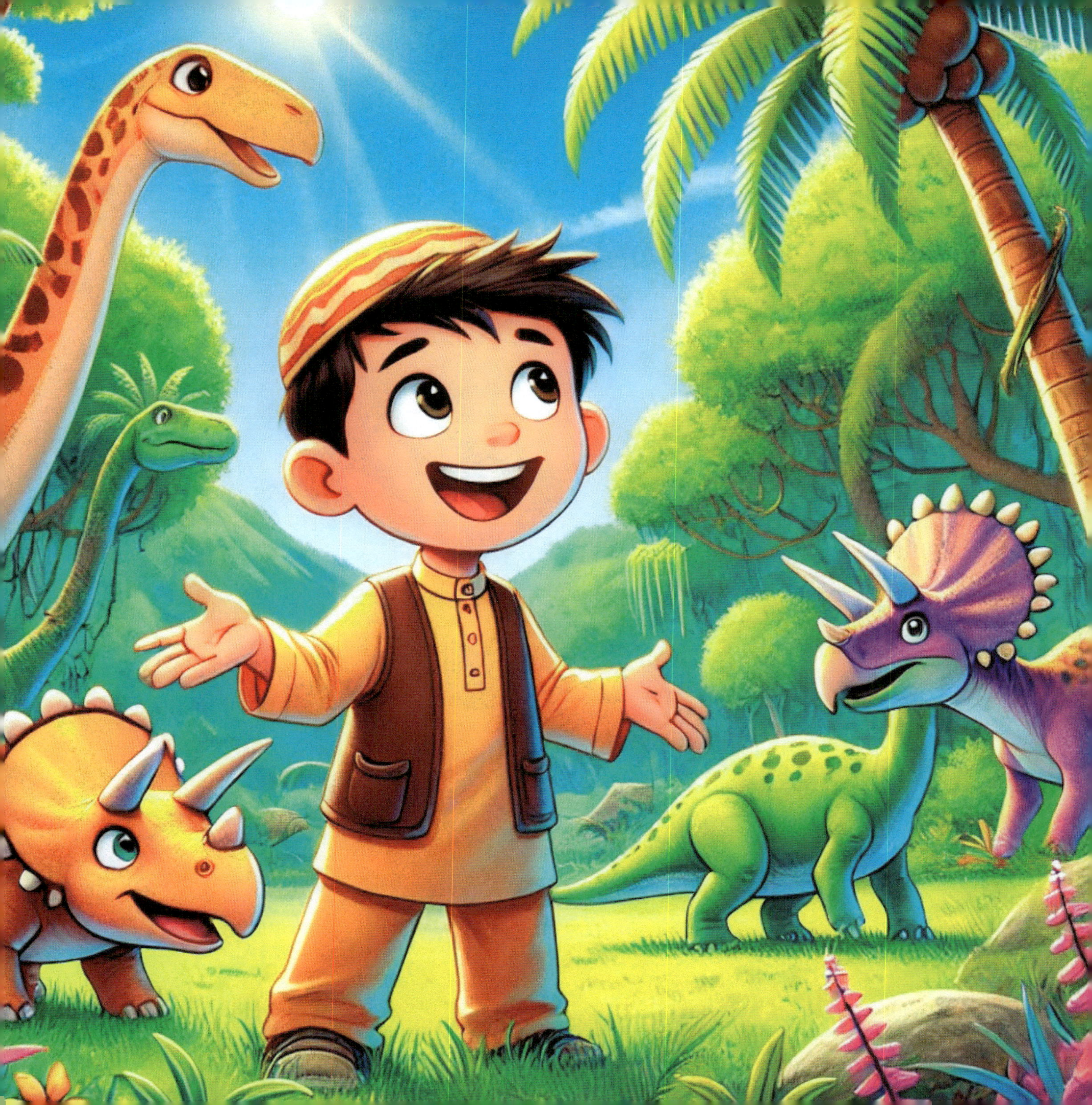

The first dinosaur he saw was a huge one with a long neck, munching on tall trees.

"Assalamu Alaikum, Mr. Dinosaur! What's your name?" Zakariyya asked.

"Wa Alaikum Assalam! I am a Brachiosaurus," said the friendly dinosaur. "I love eating leaves from the tallest trees."

Zakariyya smiled and looked up at the towering dinosaur. "You must be the tallest dinosaur in the jungle! Do you ever get scared of falling over?"

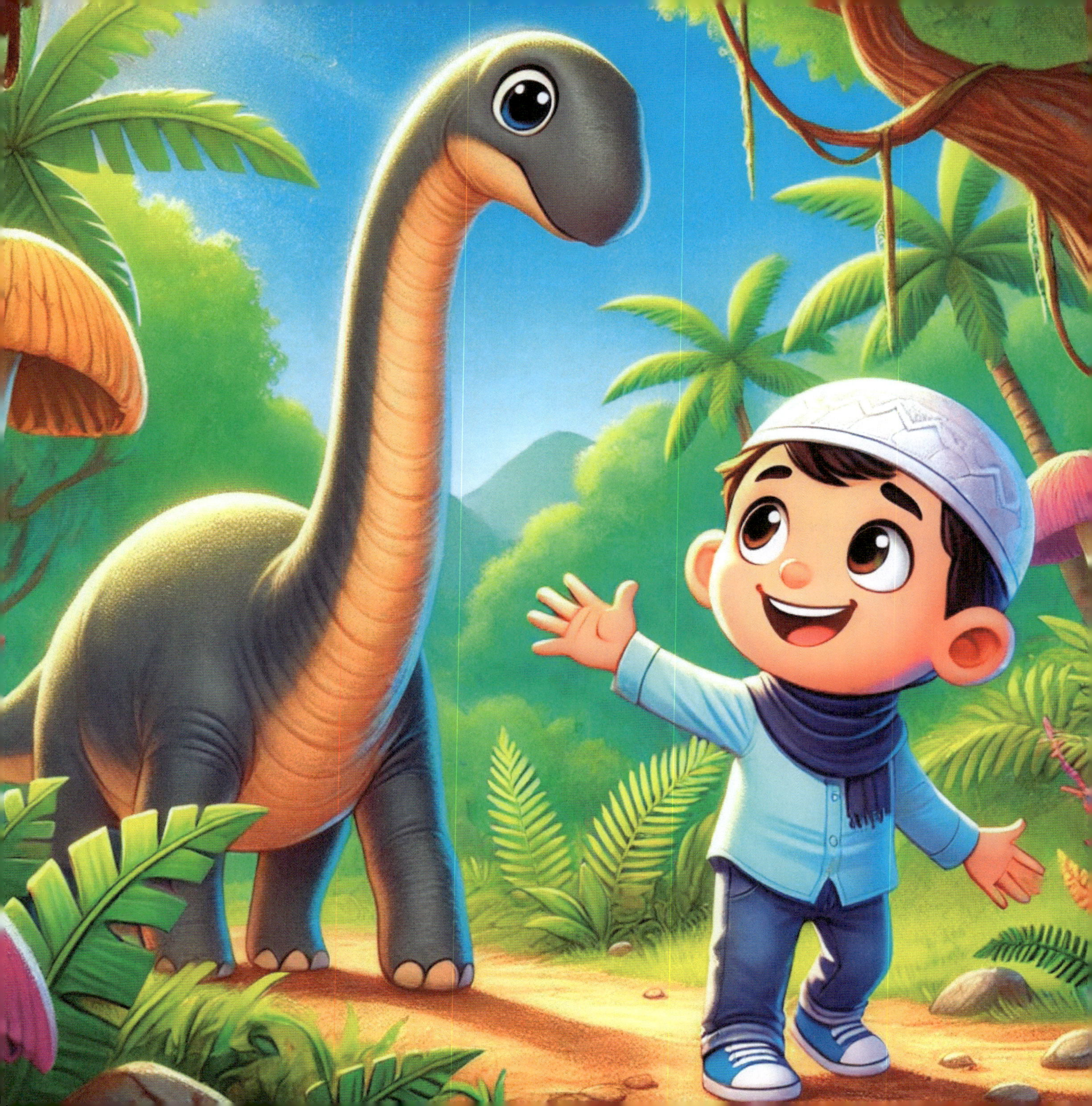

Zakariyya walked further and saw another dinosaur with three big horns on its face. "Assalamu Alaikum! Who are you?" Zakariyya asked, smiling up at the big creature.

"I am Triceratops," the dinosaur replied in a gentle voice. "I use my horns to protect myself and my friends."

Zakariyya's eyes sparkled with curiosity. "Wow! Your horns are so cool! Do you ever get scared?"

The Triceratops chuckled. "Not often, but when I do, I use my horns and my strong tail to keep danger away. But most of the time, I just enjoy eating plants and being with my herd."

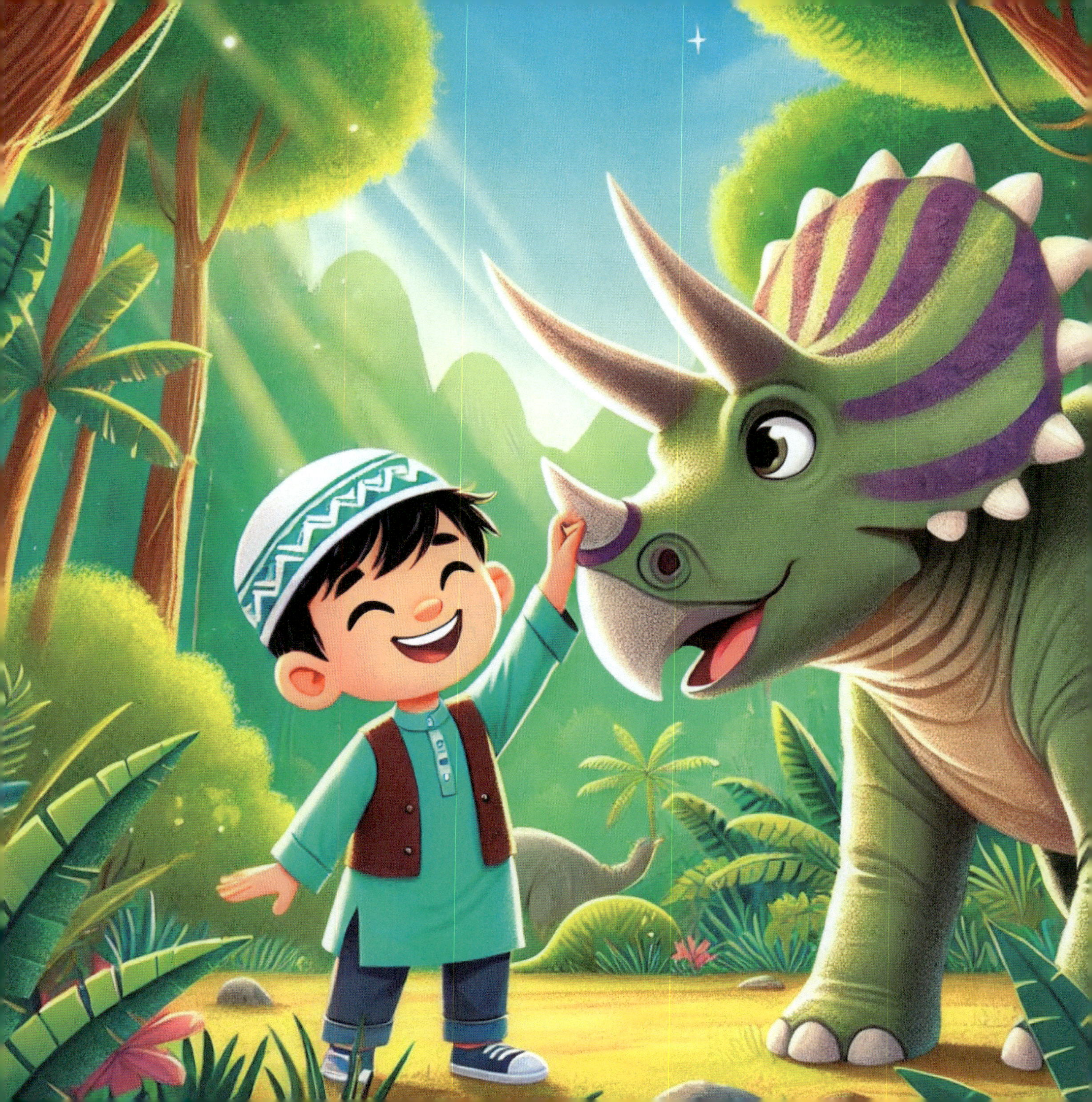

"SubhanAllah! Look at that one!" Zakariyya whispered, pointing at a Stegosaurus nearby.

The dinosaur was big and strong, with shiny, colorful plates running down its back like a row of shields. It swished its spiky tail gently as it munched on some low-hanging leaves from a bush. Zakariyya tiptoed closer, his eyes wide with wonder. The Stegosaurus looked calm and peaceful, its tiny head moving slowly as it enjoyed its snack.

Floral Cottage

Prints Pad

Floral Cottage Prints pad. Brought to you by The ScrapBooking Resource Co.

We hope you enjoy using our prints for your scrapbooking, Junk Journaling, Card Making and whatever else it may be. We would love to see your creations! You can tag us on Instagram to show us!

@Scrapbooking_Resource_Co

Floral Cottage

ScrapBooking Resource Co.

FLORAL COTTAGE

Scrapbooking Resource Co

FLORAL COTTAGE

ScrapBooking Resource Co

FLORAL COTTAGE

Scrapbooking Resource Co

FLORAL COTTAGE

ScrapBooking Resource Co

FLORAL COTTAGE

FLORAL COTTAGE

ScrapBooking Resource Co

ScrapBooking Resource Co

FLORAL COTTAGE

Floral Cottage — ScrapBooking Resource Co.

ScrapBooking Resource Co.

FLORAL COTTAGE

FLORAL COTTAGE

ScrapBooking Resource Co.

ScrapBooking Resource Co

FLORAL COTTAGE

Floral Cottage

ScrapBooking Resource Co

ScrapBooking Resource Co.

FLORAL COTTAGE

Floral Cottage — ScrapBooking Resource Co.

Floral Cottage

ScrapBooking Resource Co

FLORAL COTTAGE

ScrapBooking Resource Co

Floral Cottage

ScrapBooking Resource Co.

Floral Cottage

ScrapBooking Resource Co.

ScrapBooking Resource Co.

FLORAL COTTAGE

Floral Cottage

Scrapbooking Resource Co.

ScrapBooking Resource Co

FLORAL COTTAGE

ScrapBooking Resource Co.

FLORAL COTTAGE

ScrapBooking Resource Co.

FLORAL COTTAGE

Scrapbooking Resource Co

FLORAL COTTAGE

ScrapBooking Resource Co

FLORAL COTTAGE

ScrapBooking Resource Co

Floral Cottage

ScrapBooking Resource Co

FLORAL COTTAGE

FLORAL COTTAGE

ScrapBooking Resource Co

ScrapBooking Resource Co

FLORAL COTTAGE

FLORAL COTTAGE

ScrapBooking Resource Co

ScrapBooking Resource Co

FLORAL COTTAGE

ScrapBooking Resource Co

FLORAL COTTAGE

ScrapBooking Resource Co

FLORAL COTTAGE

Floral Cottage

ScrapBooking Resource Co

ScrapBooking Resource Co

FLORAL COTTAGE

Floral Cottage

ScrapBooking Resource Co

ScrapBooking Resource Co

FLORAL COTTAGE

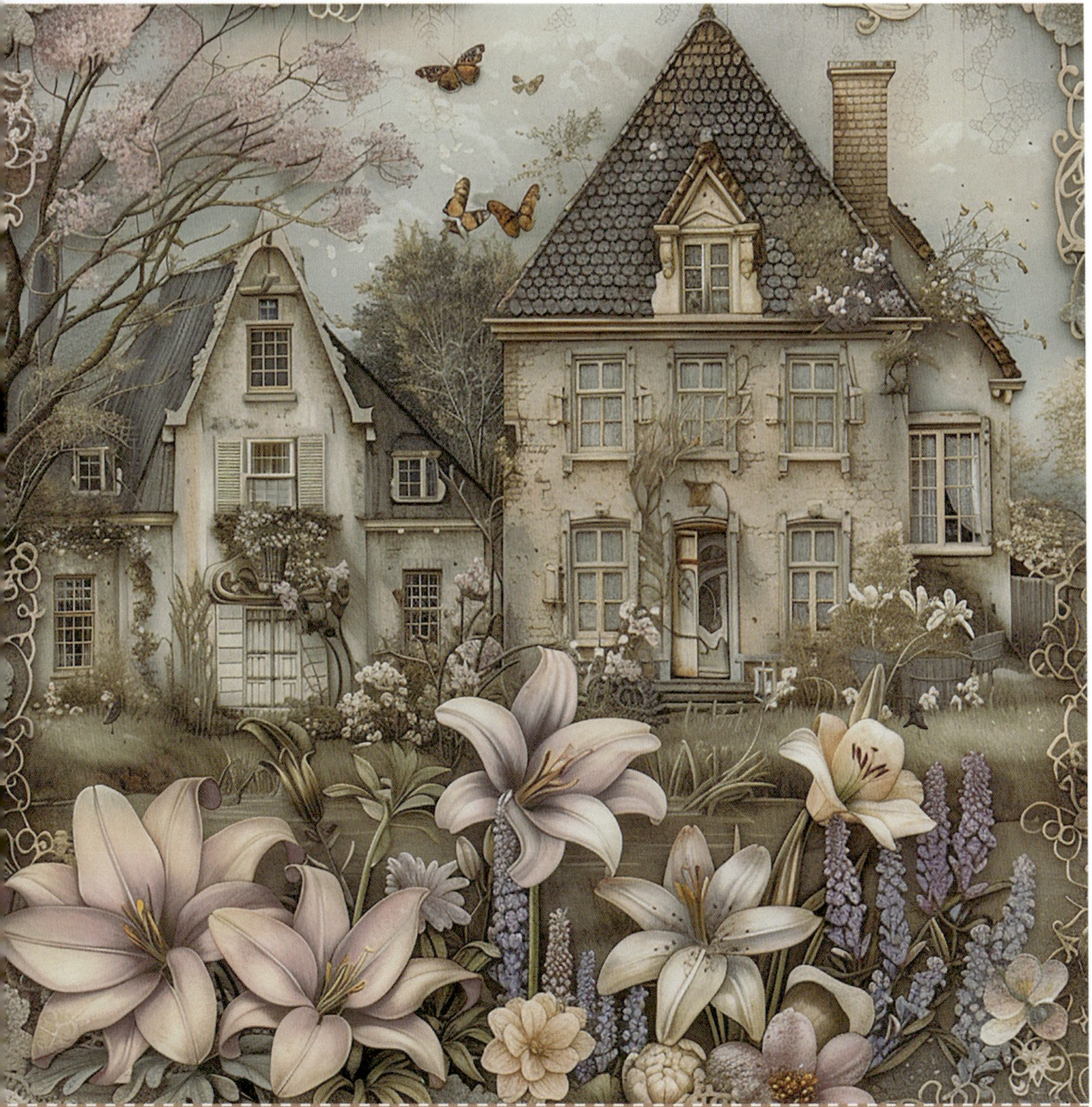

FLORAL COTTAGE

ScrapBooking Resource Co

ScrapBooking Resource Co

FLORAL COTTAGE

ScrapBooking Resource Co

FLORAL COTTAGE

ScrapBooking Resource Co

FLORAL COTTAGE

ScrapBooking Resource Co

FLORAL COTTAGE

ScrapBooking Resource Co

FLORAL COTTAGE

ScrapBooking Resource Co

FLORAL COTTAGE

ScrapBooking Resource Co

FLORAL COTTAGE

FLORAL COTTAGE

ScrapBooking Resource Co

ScrapBooking Resource Co

FLORAL COTTAGE

Floral Cottage

ScrapBooking Resource Co

ScrapBooking Resource Co

FLORAL COTTAGE

ScrapBooking Resource Co

Floral Cottage

ScrapBooking Resource Co

FLORAL COTTAGE

Scrapbooking Resource Co.

FLORAL COTTAGE

ScrapBooking Resource Co

FLORAL COTTAGE

Printed in Great Britain
by Amazon

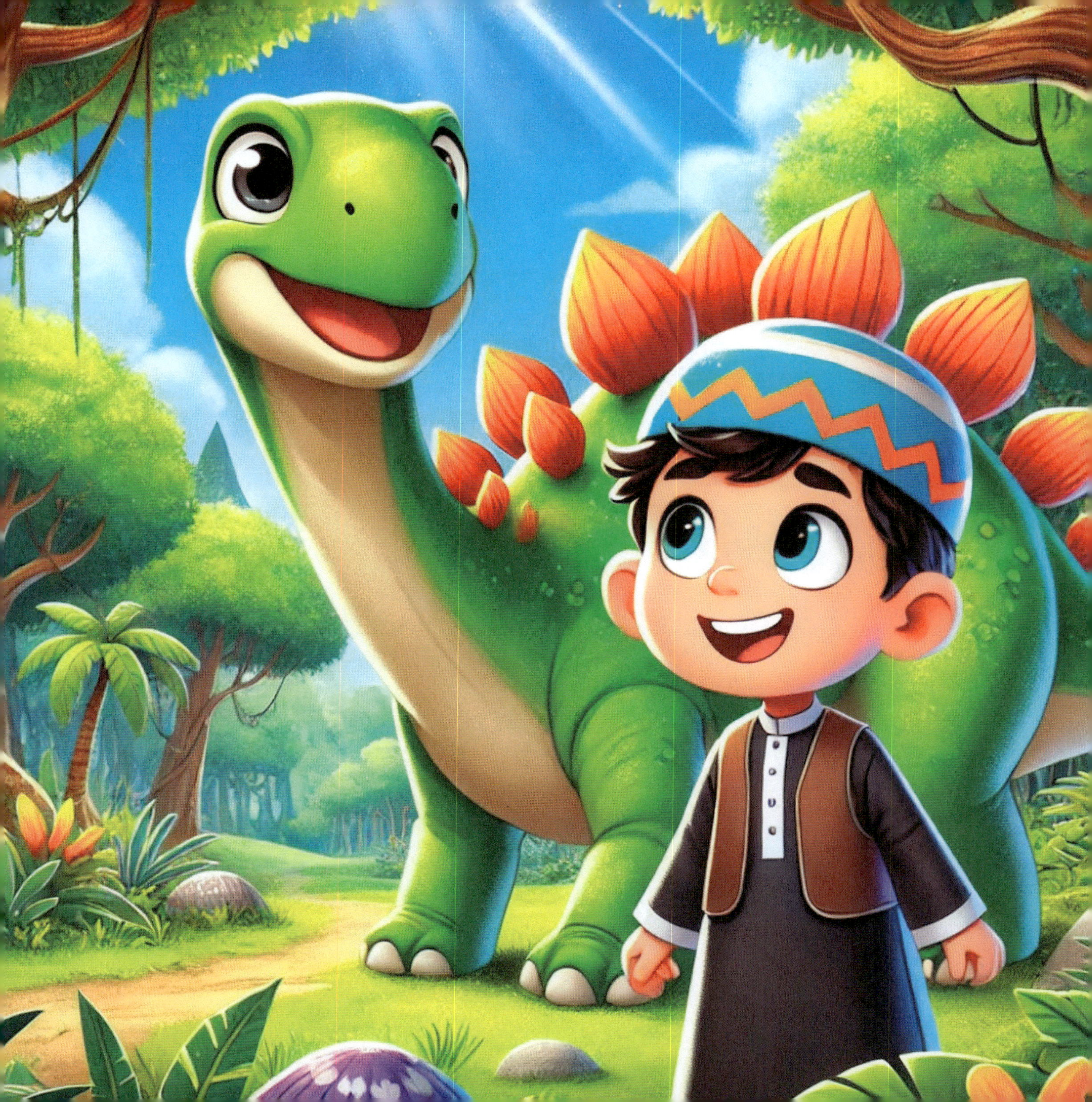

Suddenly, Zakariyya heard a loud roar! He turned around and saw the biggest dinosaur he had ever seen.

"Assalamu Alaikum! You must be very strong!" Zakariyya said bravely.

"Wa Alaikum Assalam! I am Tyrannosaurus Rex, but you can call me T-Rex," the dinosaur said with a toothy grin. "I'm a meat-eater!"

Zakariyya's eyes widened, but he felt brave. "Wow, you must be very strong! Do you ever get lonely being the king of the dinosaurs?"

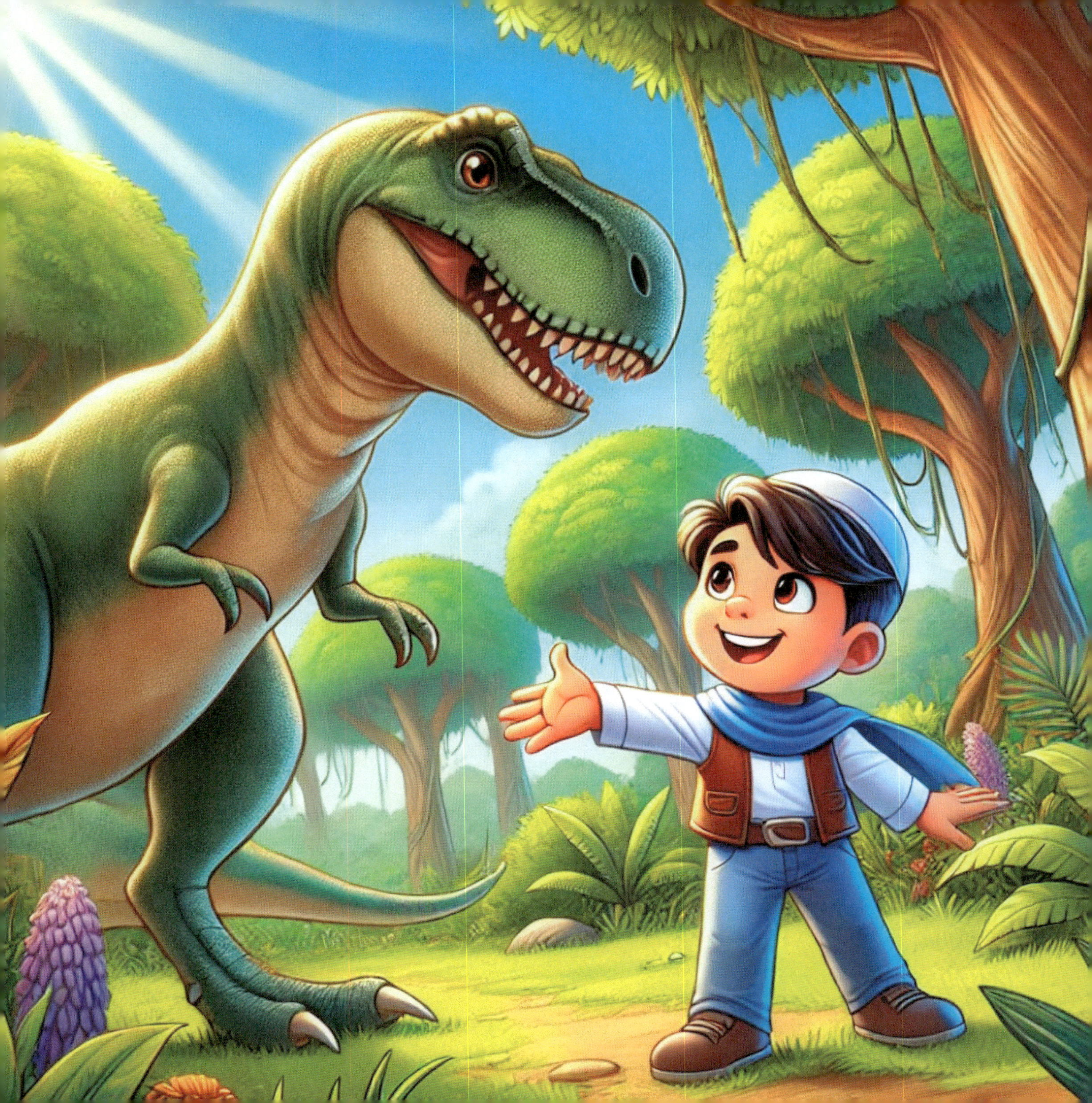

Wow! Look at that one flying!" Zakariyya exclaimed, pointing to the sky.

A huge Pterodactyl soared above the trees, its wide wings stretching out like giant sails. Its beak was long and pointed, and it let out a loud screech as it glided gracefully through the air. Zakariyya craned his neck to follow it, his mouth open in awe. "It looks like a giant bird!" he said, laughing. "I wish I could fly like that!"

The Pterodactyl swooped down low for a moment, its shadow passing over Zakariyya. He waved excitedly. "I wonder if it's friendly! Maybe it will take me for a ride!"

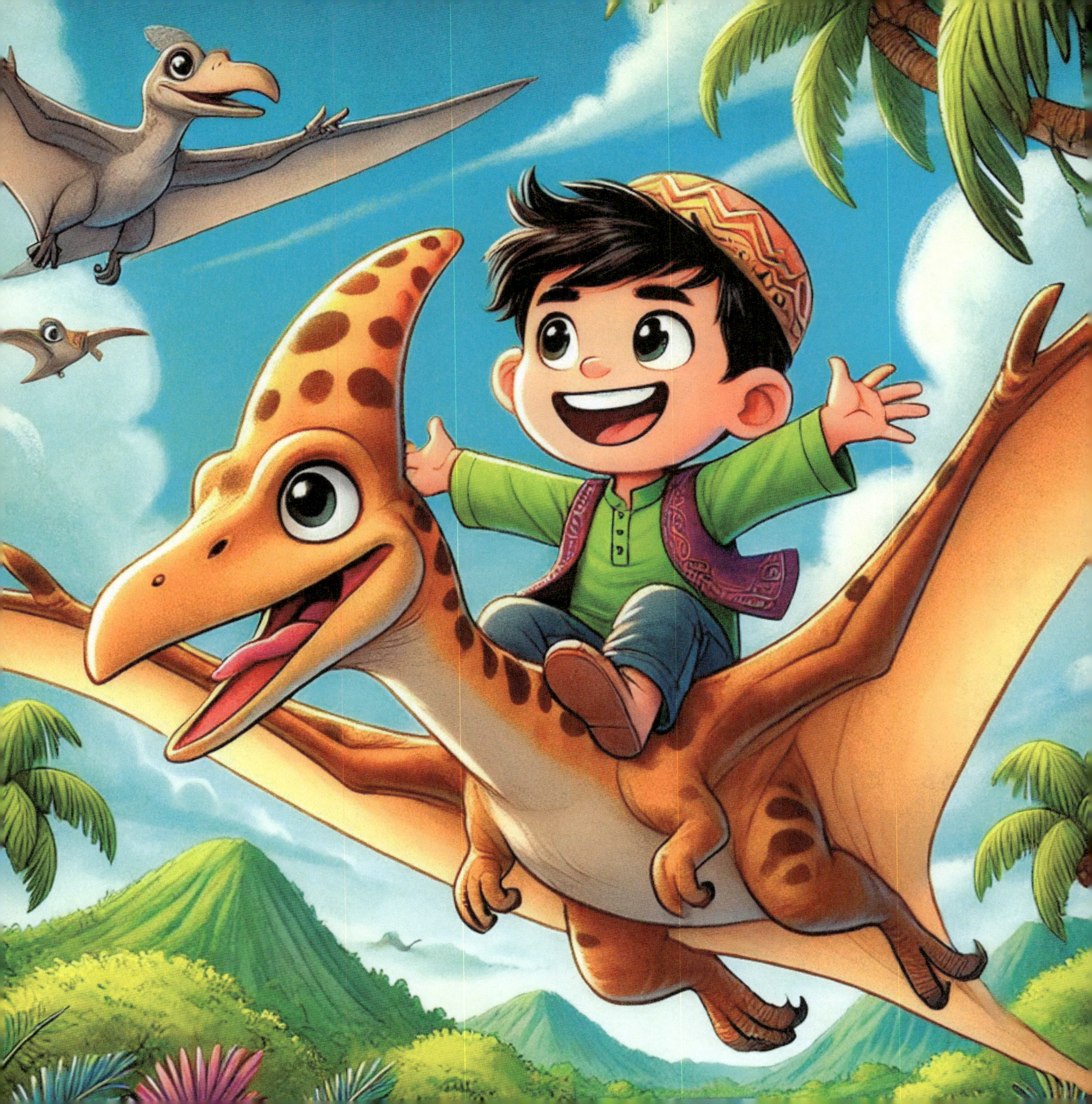

As the sun began to set, Zakariyya felt a gentle tug. It was the magic book calling him back home. "Ma'a Salama, dinosaurs! I'll never forget you!" Zakariyya waved goodbye.

Zakariyya opened his eyes and found himself back in his room. The adventure was over, but the memories stayed in his heart. He ran to Daddy. "Daddy, Alhamdulillah, that was an exciting adventure. I love you so much. One day, I'll be a dinosaur explorer, InshaAllah!"

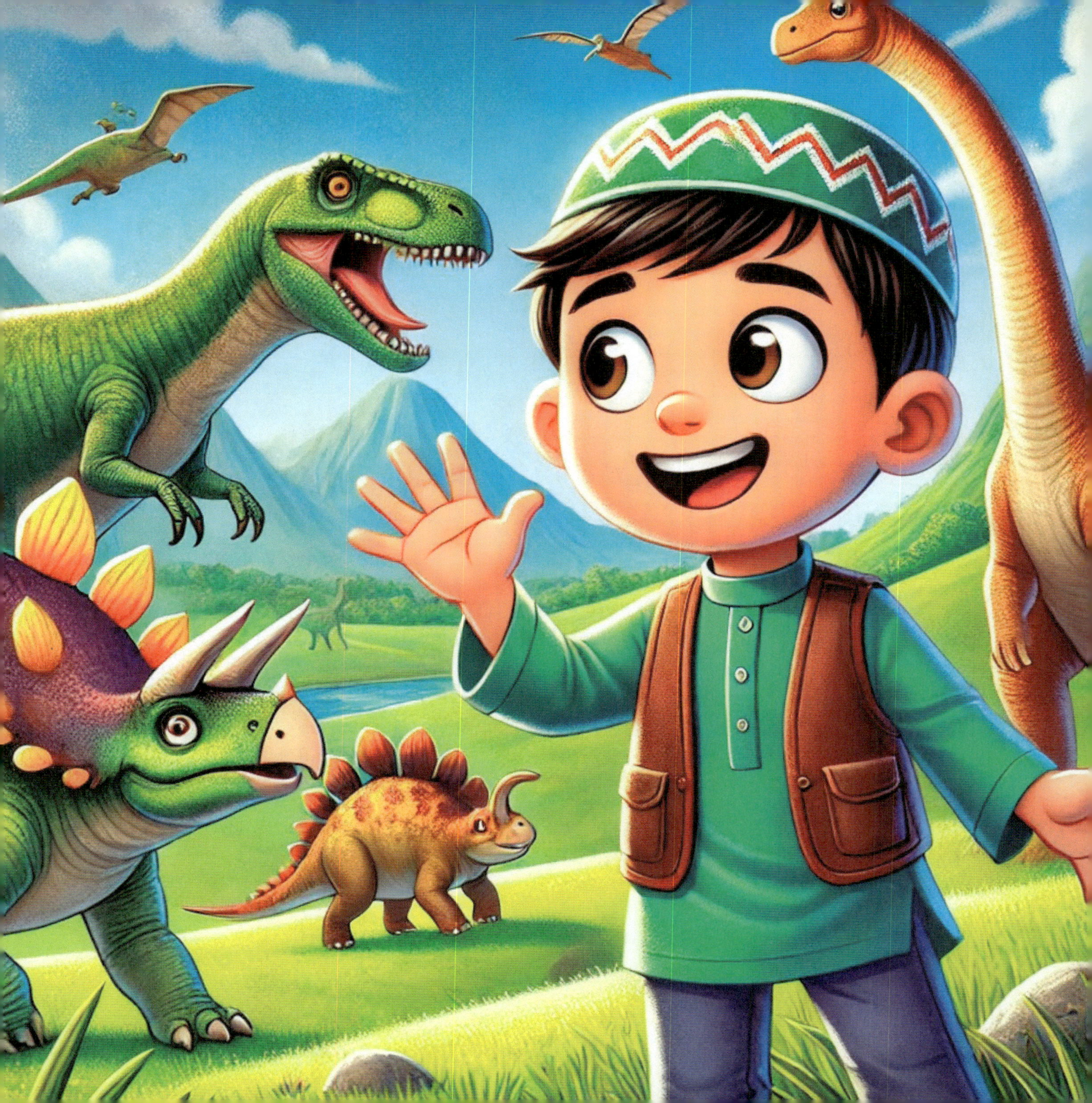

A MESSAGE ABOUT PARENTAL ALIENATION

Dear Parents,

As parents, our primary goal is to nurture our children with love, stability and support. In the midst of life's challenges, it is crucial to remember that our actions and words have a profound impact on their emotional well-being, especially when it comes to their relationship with both parents.

Parental alienation, whether intentional or unintentional, can harm a child's ability to form healthy connections and affect their emotional growth. When we speak negatively about the other parent, limit access or undermine their role, it puts our children in a difficult position. They may feel torn, conflicted, or even pressured to "choose sides," which can lead to feelings of guilt, anxiety and sadness.

Every child deserves a healthy, loving relationship with both parents whenever it is safe and possible. Studies consistently show that children thrive when they have the active involvement of both parents in their lives. A child's love for one parent does not diminish their love for the other—just as their bond with one parent does not negate the importance of the other.

As challenging as it may be during conflicts or transitions, let us commit to placing the best interests of our children above all else. This means fostering respect for the other parent's role, ensuring open communication where possible and encouraging our children to maintain meaningful connections with both of parents.

By focusing on our children's emotional health and needs, we can help them grow into resilient, confident, and loving individuals. Let us be united in this shared responsibility of giving them the best foundation for a happy and balanced future.

With care and understanding,
Waqas Amin
14.12.2024

Printed in Great Britain
by Amazon